4/07

**KIDS &
COMPUTERS**

Kids & Computers

The Big Machines

Charles A. Jortberg

Published by Abdo & Daughters, 4940 Viking Drive, Suite 622, Edina, Minnesota 55435.

Copyright © 1997 by Abdo Consulting Group, Inc., Pentagon Tower, P.O. Box 36036, Minneapolis, Minnesota 55435 USA. International copyrights reserved in all countries. No part of this book may be reproduced in any form without written permission from the publisher.

Printed in the United States.

Cover and Interior Photo credits: Wide World Photos
                                            Archive Photos
                                            Jortberg Associates
                                            Super Stock
                                            Bettmann Archive

Edited by John Hamilton

Library of Congress Cataloging-in-Publication Data

Jortberg, Charles A.
   The big machines / Charles A. Jortberg.
     p. cm. -- (Kids and computers)
   Includes index.
   Summary: Describes the explosive growth of computers in the world over the past forty-five years and their uses in business, communication, air traffic control, and the space program.
   ISBN 1-56239-725-7
   1. Computers--Juvenile literature. [1. Computers.] I. Title. II. Series: Jortberg, Charles A. Kids and computers.
QA76.52.J67 1997
004.1'2--dc20

                                                         96-28297
                                                            CIP
                                                             AC

About the Author

Charles A. Jortberg graduated from Bowdoin College in 1951 with a Bachelor's Degree in Economics. Mr. Jortberg joined IBM in 1954 and served in several capacities. Among his assignments were coordinating all of IBM's efforts with the Air Force, managing a 20-person team of IBM engineers, and directing a number of technical programs at NASA's Electronic Research Laboratory. He formed Jortberg Associates in 1972, where he currently works, to provide an outlet for his start-up technology experience.

Contents

RCA and IBM

The growth in the number of computers in the world over the past 45 years has been explosive. This growth has been compared to the huge increase in the number of automobiles since Henry Ford invented the assembly line, or number of color television sets sold since they were invented by RCA.

In 1953, a scientist at IBM predicted that the entire world would only need 100 computers. (How wrong can a person be?) Today, with microprocessors in nearly every car, airplane, office, laboratory, and school, there are over 100 million programmable processors in use.

After World War II, as U. S. industry switched from making weapons to making products, there was a great period of business growth. New cars were produced again, washers and dryers were in great demand, millions of new houses were constructed, and new furniture was needed to fill those homes.

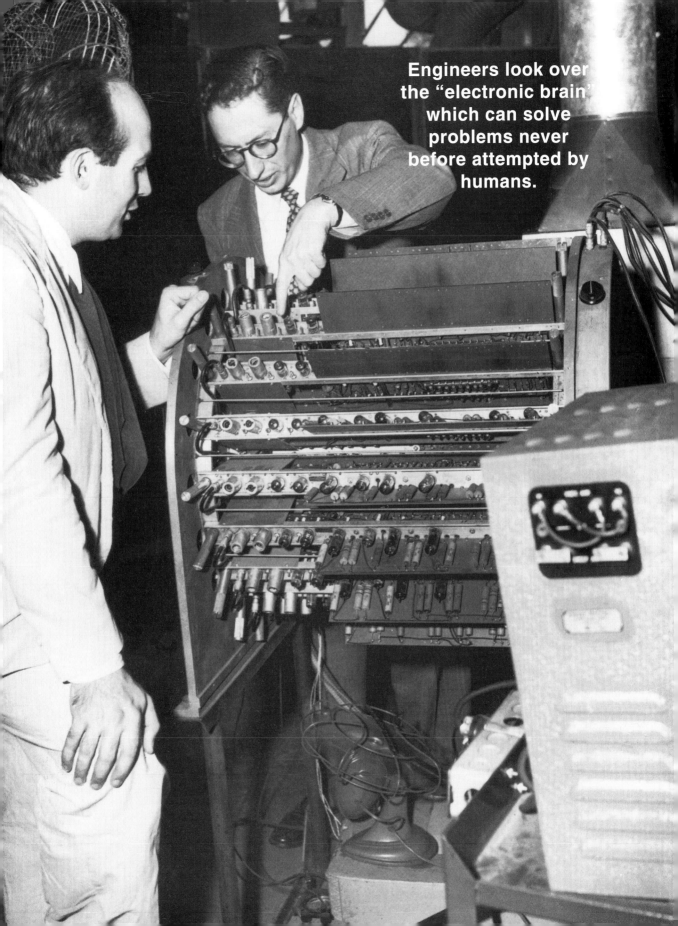

Engineers look over the "electronic brain" which can solve problems never before attempted by humans.

Companies such as IBM, Remington Rand, Burroughs, and National Cash Register grew rapidly, producing business machines to support the boom in business.

During this time, there were exciting new developments at Harvard University, the Massachusetts Institute of Technology, Princeton, the University of Pennsylvania, and other locations. Under the directions of people like Howard Aiken at Harvard, and John Eckert and John Mauchly at the University of Pennsylvania, exciting new computers were demonstrated. These experimental systems were huge, and could be used only by the most highly-trained scientists.

The complexity, size, and costs of the experimental computers were the main reasons people felt there would never be a large number installed. The rush to bring these large-scale ideas to reality came from a combination of world events that nearly started another World War.

The Rush to Build a Big Computer

During the years following World War II, the United States, the former Soviet Union (U.S.S.R.), and their allies struggled to control Eastern Europe. Each side felt threatened, leading to a huge military buildup. This struggle became known as the "Cold War."

With the aid of German scientists who had designed guided missile systems for the Nazis, the Soviets quickly developed missiles that could travel thousands of miles. Missiles could be launched from deep within the U.S.S.R. and land on cities in the United States. The United States responded by building its own guided missiles, aiming them at major cities in the Soviet Union. In addition to missiles, the United States and the U.S.S.R. each had fleets of long-range bombers that carried atomic weapons able to destroy entire cities.

To detect an enemy launch of missiles or bombers, the United States decided to build an electronic "wall" that would warn people of an attack. Since an attack would most likely travel over the Arctic Circle on its way to the United States, a group of huge radar screens was built in northern Canada. (The U.S.S.R. also built its own array of radar screens in northern Siberia.) This group of radar screens was called the "Dew Line." DEW stood for Distant Early Warning System.

Satellite dishes that pick up sound waves from all over the world.

The DEW Line

When the DEW line was built, it created a need for quickly finding out where an attack was coming from, where it would hit, and what defenses could be used to protect the people in the target area. Plans were made to build a huge computer system that could receive all these radar signals, determine what was attacking, and where it was headed.

This new computer system was named SAGE. Plans were made to build several SAGE computers and place them in important locations all over the United States. The U.S. Air Force worked closely with scientists from the Massachusetts Institute of Technology and IBM to design a computer system that would receive the information from the DEW line and other radar locations. This computer system would compute the type of attack, where it was aimed, and issue attack warnings.

Each SAGE computer was also linked to a network of radar stations. If radar detected an airplane, the computer searched the records of all U.S. military and commercial flights. In seconds, the SAGE system could decide if the aircraft was supposed to be where the radar showed. If there were strange airplanes in the area, the SAGE computer would "scramble" U.S. fighter jets to check them out.

The SAGE computers were huge. Entire buildings were constructed to house them. The heat from these computers helped warm the buildings in which they were located.

The Air Force computer operators were seated at displays that looked like big TV sets and had so many buttons and switches they looked like spaceships. Each display had a map of a certain part of the United States. Any time an object was sensed by radar, it appeared on the screen as a "blip," or small bit of light. When the object moved, the "blip" moved—and the Air Force could see where it was going.

If the "blip" turned out to be suspicious, the Air Force scrambled its jets. For many years the SAGE computer systems provided a shield against attack.

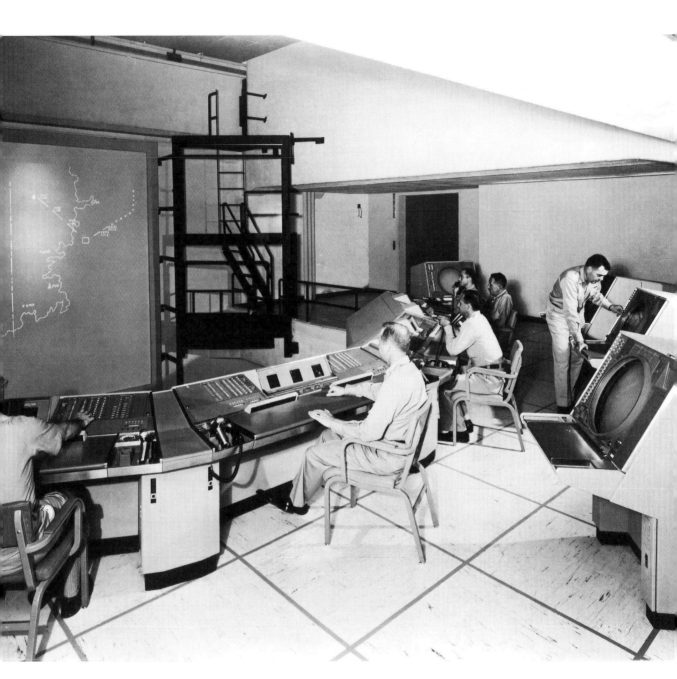

The SAGE (Semi-Automatic Ground Environment) system.

What Makes a Computer Work

The major elements of the SAGE computer are the same elements used today in nearly all digital computers in the world.

This engineer programmed one of the first investment portfolios for IBM.

Programming

Every single thing you want a computer to do must be given in the form of "instructions." All the instructions you give a computer to solve a problem is called a "computer program."

Before you write a program, it is necessary to make detailed plans of what you want to do. Many people produce what is known as a "block diagram," where each step is described in detail so that computer instructions can later be written that will complete the step.

For the early computers, programmers wrote instructions in "machine language." This was a very tiresome job. Everything had to be written as a series of 1's or 0's. Then the computer changed the language to electrical signals, which performed the proper instructions. Programs took a long time to write, and often had many errors.

Major improvements soon increased the speed and accuracy of computer programs. These improvements included the invention of the compiler. A compiler is a program that translates English-like sentences or arithmetic statements into the proper 1's and 0's.

Another important part of the programming world is the "operating system." This program keeps track of everything that is going on in the computer. It keeps track of memory, schedules all the pieces of the computer, checks on the progress of all programs, and performs several other tasks.

Processor

The processor is the heart of the computer. It is often made of three major sections—the CPU, the control section, and the memory. These are located side-by-side in most computers, and are connected by wires or cables.

The brain of any computer is the central processing unit, often called the CPU. The CPU does all the arithmetic needed to solve a problem, including addition, subtraction, multiplication, and division. All calculations are done millions of times every second. The CPU can compare two things to see if they are the same, or if one is larger or smaller than the other.

The control section controls the flow of information in the computer. Computers must store this information so that the CPU can work with it. This storage is called memory. Memory also stores computer programs and the data these programs need to complete their tasks.

There are two types of memory: internal and auxiliary. Internal memory is located in the CPU. As the CPU processes data and instructions, it temporarily stores this information in its memory. Internal memory is very fast, which allows the CPU to do millions of tasks every second.

THE COMPUTER PROCESSOR

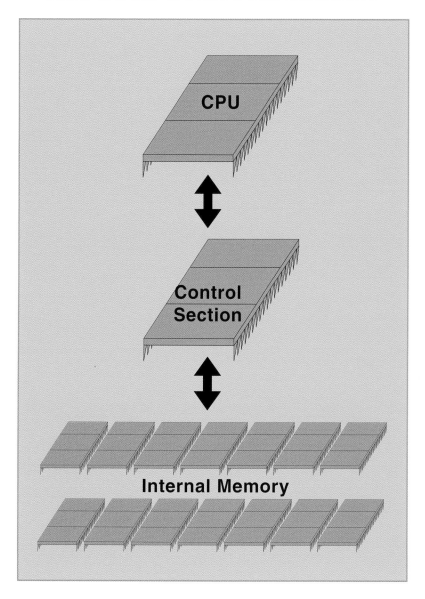

The computer processor is made of three main parts: the CPU, the control section, and the internal memory. The control section controls the flow of information between the CPU (where information is processed) and the internal memory (where information is stored).

Auxiliary memory is located outside the CPU. This memory stores instructions and data that cannot fit in the internal memory.

Auxiliary memory comes in many forms. Many of today's personal computers use small disks that measure only 3.5 x 5 inches (9 x 13 cm) and can easily fit into a shirt pocket. These are known as "floppy" disks because the first ones were made of soft plastic that could easily bend. Most "floppy" disks are now made of stiffer plastic and don't bend, but the name is still used. Each of these small disks can store millions of numbers or letters, which the processor can transfer into and out of internal memory.

Many times, a computer needs to update information. A good example is school records, where grades are

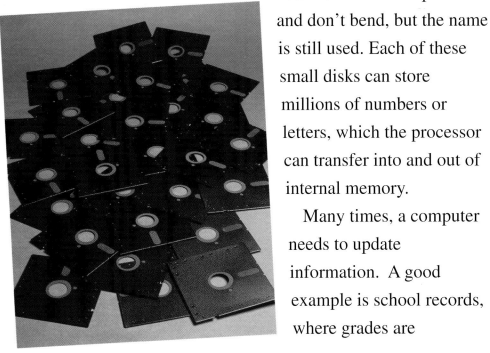

The five-inch floppy disk.

This disk drive records and plays back thousands of pages of information from a computer.

compiled. The computer transfers old records from a disk to the internal memory, adds the new grades, then returns the updated records to the disk.

When data is transferred from auxiliary to internal memory, it is "read." When the computer transfers data from internal to auxiliary memory, it is "written." The large computers use bigger disk storage systems where the disks cannot be removed. These "hard disks" can store billions of numbers and letters. Information from these bigger disks is also moved in and out of the internal memory when the CPU needs it.

These disks can store over 2 billion characters of information. All the words in the books shown can go onto these three disks.

IBM 701 tape drives.

Another form of outside memory is magnetic tape. Big computer systems have units called tape drives, on which large reels of magnetic tape are mounted. These reels contain over half a mile of tape similar to the tape in your cassette player. Instead of music, these tapes contain data for the CPU. This data is transferred over cable or wires into the internal memory when the CPU needs it. These reels of tapes can be removed, so hundreds of tape reels can be stored in rooms called libraries, and only used when needed.

The U.S. Government uses thousands of reels of tape containing the personal information of every person in the United States who works and pays taxes. These tapes are updated several times a year as the information changes.

Every computer needs several ways to obtain and store information. Older computers read information from punched cards. Punched cards stored data before computers existed. For each number or letter, one or two holes would be punched in a card that was about the size of a dollar bill. Each card could contain eighty numbers or letters. When the first big computers needed data, a machine read these cards at a very slow rate. The SAGE system needed 60,000 to enter one program. If these cards were placed end to end, they would stretch from the ground to an airplane flying at 30,000 feet (9,144 m).

Displays

Modern large computers are equipped with many methods of entering data. Many computers have hundreds of display stations connected to the CPU with telephone lines or cables. These display stations have keyboards and screens that look like small televisions. You can sit at one of these terminals and enter data on the keyboard and then look at it on the screen. If the data is correct, pushing a button will send it to the CPU, which can be in the next room or thousands of miles away.

These displays can also show pictures and graphics. For example, an automobile designer can sit in front of a computer display about the size of a 25-inch TV and "enter" a new car style. Using a device that looks like a pen with a cable on the

IBM personal computer with a display.

end, the designer can "draw" sketches on the screen. The computer traces the sketches and calculates exactly what they should look like, then draws final pictures that look like photographs.

Many police departments use color displays to help identify crime suspects. An eyewitness can describe to an officer what the suspect looks like, and the officer can enter this description on the keyboard of the display. The computer searches its memory until it finds a matching picture which it displays on the screen. From this picture, a printer can produce copies that can be sent to other police departments.

A customer-operated checkout computer in a
grocery store.

Many stores are equipped with small display units that can read information from plastic credit cards. When you buy something, the name and price of the item is sent to a computer. Later on, this same computer can send you a bill for the item you bought and record your payment.

Many grocery stores have a fast way of entering data into a central computer, which has a record of everything in the store, including the name and number of the item, its price, and how many the store has on the shelves. Each package has several small printed lines called a "bar code." Each bar code represents the item number stored in the computer memory.

When you go through the checkout, the person at the cash register drags the item over a glass pane that has a special reader below it. This reader reads the bar code and sends the number to the computer. The computer then sends the price to the cashier. The name of the product is printed on a receipt where the groceries are totaled.

Sending Messages

Computer display stations can be located thousands of miles from the computer and send data or receive pictures as if they were sitting in the same room. This is done by sending electrical signals over the same telephone lines used to call friends or family in faraway cities. The information in the computer is changed to the same type of signal used by the telephone lines, and the information travels on the lines until it reaches the display station. Then the signal is changed to the type the computer uses.

This same kind of communication is used when one computer sends a message to another computer. Special telephone circuits can carry millions of numbers and letters every minute. Sometimes the information is sent from one location to another by way of a satellite. The letters and numbers are sent up to the satellite and then down to another location in millionths of a second.

Printers

When a computer finishes a task, it often prints out the results in many shapes and forms. Computers print paychecks, report cards, detailed designs of new cars, and thousands of other things. Computer printers can produce thousands of lines every minute and in several colors. There are printers that also draw detailed house plans, pictures of distant galaxies, and schoolbooks.

Weather pictures from a satellite are transmitted to a small printer at a ground station.

Applications

Large computers perform a number of exciting applications that capture our imagination and provide a range of services for our everyday life.

Air Traffic Control

In addition to protecting the United States against military attack, the SAGE system provided many other benefits that have lasted to this day. When SAGE proved that radar could track the flight of airplanes and show them on a computer display screen, the U.S. government decided to build the same type of system to keep track of the hundreds of commercial airplanes that were crowding the skies.

In the air traffic control system, a network of air traffic control centers keeps track of all aircraft within a certain region. Each region is comprised of four to six states. The radar at each center feeds data to its computer, including the number of a flight, its altitude, speed, and destination. Each plane must fly only at the altitude assigned by the air traffic control center. The computers at these centers are actually setting up "highways in the sky."

As a plane continues on its journey, the air traffic computers keep track of its progress, alerting the pilot to any weather problems on the route. If an airplane runs into a storm or choppy air, the pilot can ask the computer for permission to fly at another altitude where the weather might be better. Planes are

A Federal Aviation Administration controller checks his scope at the FAA air route traffic control center.

not allowed to change direction without permission. The air traffic control computers keep track of all weather conditions with information from the Weather Bureau, radar, and other planes. If severe weather develops, such as a thunderstorm, the computer can warn planes in its area and direct them in a path that will take them around the problems.

When a plane is about to leave the air space of one computer center, it is "passed off" to a new center. When this happens, all the computer records of the flight are sent to the new computer over telephone lines. The telephone lines pass along the information at thousands of numbers and letters each second.

Each major airport also has complex radar systems that are tied into computers similar to the air traffic control centers. When a plane nears its destination, it is then "handed off" from the air traffic control center to the computer at the airport. There, air traffic controllers sit in front of huge computer displays. As in the original SAGE system, each of these displays shows a map of the area around the airport. Each airplane in the area is shown as a "blip" with the flight number on the screen. The air traffic controllers keep track of thousands of planes each day, and with the displays they make sure there are no collisions.

The weather service checks weather around the world to help airplanes fly around weather problems.

NASA

When the United States undertook its major space program under President John F. Kennedy, many of the original lessons learned in the SAGE program were put to work. NASA built several tracking systems all over the world with radar so strong they could sense any activity in outer space. These radar stations were connected with telephone lines and satellite links to huge computer systems at the Manned Space Center in Houston, Texas. When satellites were launched from Cape Canaveral in Florida, or from other locations in California, the radar signals "tracked" them. The path of each orbit was shown on wall-size display screens that also displayed maps of the world and the progress of the satellite.

Computers also keep track of thousands of items of space "junk." For the past 30 years there have been hundreds of satellites launched into orbit. Many lost their usefulness as their batteries wore out or they fell apart. This floating "junk" can be very dangerous if a spaceship runs into them. Therefore, NASA computers must keep careful track of this hazardous "junk."

The role of computers at NASA starts long before a blast-off occurs. Each flight is planned in detail in the giant computers, and the schedule is set up for every split second of the mission. Before a mission starts, the computer is programmed to run through every step of what is going to happen. This is called "simulation." The giant computers are connected to life-size models of the spacecraft, and the astronauts are trained in every aspect of a flight without leaving the ground. The computers can also create fake emergencies, so the astronauts can learn what to do when they are in danger.

NASA Mercury Control Center, Cape Canaveral, Florida.

The giant NASA computers are also used to receive pictures from outer space. When spacecraft like *Galileo* approach faraway planets like Jupiter, they use cameras that send radio signals back to gigantic tracking stations on earth. These radio signals are then processed by the computer systems to produce high-quality photographs. The Hubble Space Telescope is now sending back radio signals that show events which happened thousands of years ago in space. These radio signals are also used by supercomputer systems to create pictures of distant galaxies that have never been seen before.

In addition to the exciting uses of computers in the space program and air traffic control, many businesses use these big computers to keep track of employees, inventory records, and for hundreds of other applications. The U.S. Government became the largest user of computers in the world with its machines in the Census Bureau, the Social Security Administration, and many other departments.

Kennedy Space Center, Florida. The firing room during the *Apollo 4* mission. The electronic "brain" of Launch Complex 39A.

Glossary

Air Traffic Control System - A network of air traffic control centers; controls flights of all aircraft in the U.S.

bar code - A series of printed bars that represent numbers or letters and can be scanned into computers.

blip - An electronic image on a radar screen representing an object sensed by radar.

Central Processing Unit (CPU) - The brain of the computer; the CPU does all the arithmetic needed to solve a problem, including addition, subtraction, multiplication, and division. All calculations are done millions of times every second. The CPU can compare two things to see if they are the same, or if one is larger or smaller than the other.

Cold War - The fight for control of Europe after World War II by Russia, other European nations, and the United States.

compiler - A program that translates English into the proper 1's and 0's.

computer - An electronic device that performs complex mathematical calculations quickly, using information and instructions it receives and stores.

computer program - The total set of instructions used to solve a particular problem.

control section - The part of the computer where all the control circuits are located. The control section controls the flow of information in the computer.

disk drive - A device that rotates a magnetic storage disk, can record data on the disk, and can read data from the disk.

display station - Work stations connected to the CPU (Central Processing Unit) via telephone lines or cables.

Distant Early Warning System (DEW Line) - A series of radar stations located in Canada used to detect an enemy launch of missiles or bombers.

floppy disks - A form of outside computer memory. The first disks were made of a soft "floppy" plastic.

magnetic tape - A form of outside memory. Larger computers had units called tape drives where large reels of magnetic tape were mounted to retrieve or store information.

memory - An area in the computer where information is stored. Memory also stores computer programs and the data these programs need to complete their tasks.

NASA - National Aeronautics and Space Administration. A federal agency established by the U.S. Congress in 1958 to supervise U.S. space activities for peaceful purposes.

NATO - North Atlantic Treaty Association. A Western alliance providing for joint action in an attack against any member. It also promotes joint military aid and economic cooperation during peace time.

operating system - A program that keeps track of all computer functions. It keeps track of memory, schedules all the pieces of the computer, checks on the progress of all programs, and performs several other tasks.

printers - A device that expresses coded characters as hard copy.

processor - The heart of the computer. It is often made of three major sections: the CPU, the control section, and the memory. These are located side-by-side in most computers, and are connected by wires or cables.

program - A series of coded instructions used to direct a computer in the solution of a problem.

programmer - A person who programs a computer.

programming - Preparing instructions for a computer.

punched card system - A system that uses punched cards to store information and computer programs.

radar - A method of detecting the position, speed, and other characteristics of a distant object by analyzing the radio waves reflected from the object's surface.

SAGE - A large computer system linked to the DEW line that received all radar signals and determined where an attack was headed.

simulation - A computer representation of a real-life system or process that imitates the behavior of the real system under a variety of conditions.

Index